Fulfilling Your Personal Prophecy

Dr. Bill Hamon

CHRISTIAN INTERNATIONAL
P.O. Box 9000
Santa Rosa Beach, FL 32549-9000

Printed in the United States of America
ISBN 0-939868-07-5

Introduction

There is a move in the Church today by the Holy Spirit to bring clarity and understanding about the role of the prophet and prophetic ministry. With this present move is a tremendous rise in personal prophetic ministry and a hunger in the hearts of God's people to fulfill all that the Lord has revealed to them.

Because of this, the intent of this book is to share vital prophetic principles for properly responding to God's voice in personal prophecy. The majority of this material was taken from *Prophets and Personal Prophecy Vol. 1* by the same author, Dr. Bill Hamon.

Our prayer is that this timely information helps you to properly respond and fulfill personal prophecies you have received or will receive.

Fulfilling Your Personal Prophecy

Most Christian theologians and preachers agree that there were many prophets in the Old Testament. All agree that they were God's main means of communicating His specific desires and purposes for mortals on planet Earth. But some theologians, because of their lack of proper biblical understanding and life experience with prophets and the Prophetic Movement, have made statements that questioned the validity of prophets and prophetic ministry within the New Testament Church. They developed strange doctrines which implied that the establishment of the New Testament somehow

1

did away with the need for prophets and the prophetic ministry.

The coming of the Holy Spirit, the birth of the Church, and the writing of the Bible did not eliminate the need for the prophetic voice of the Lord; in fact it intensified that need. Peter insisted that the prophet Joel was speaking of the Church age when he proclaimed, "I will pour out my Spirit in those days, and your sons and daughters shall prophesy" (Acts 2:17). Paul emphasized that truth when he told the church at Corinth to "covet to prophesy" (I Cor. 14:39; Eph. 4:11).

God still wants the revelation of His will to be vocalized, so He has established the prophetic ministry as a voice of revelation and illumination which will reveal the mind of Christ to the human race. He also uses this ministry to give specific instructions to individuals concerning His personal will for their lives. Of course, the ministry of the prophet is

2

not to bring about additions or subtractions to the Bible but to bring illumination and further specifics about that which has already been written.

This booklet is written to those who have received a prophetic word and desire to understand how to properly respond to it so that it might come to fruition. This is not to say that personal prophecy should ever become a personal substitute for an individual's responsibility and privilege of hearing the voice of God for himself. God is not pleased when we allow anything to hinder an intimate relationship and personal communication with Him - even if the hindrance is from a ministry He Himself has ordained. But once we have received a "personal word" from the Lord, it is our obligation to comprehend how to properly respond to God's voice.

For this reason I would like to share with you six prophetic principles for properly responding

3

to God's voice. I have learned these vital truths from over 39 years of experience in prophetic ministry.

Most Christians do not realize that the person receiving a personal prophecy has as much responsibility to rightly respond as the prophet has in giving a right word. In fact there are many more biblical examples of prophecies failing to come to pass because of an improper response than there are failures because the prophecy was false. Please keep in mind while studying these principles, the biblical premise that personal prophecy is always conditional whether conditional terms are used or certain requirements are specified.

SIX PRINCIPLES OF PROPER RESPONSE TO THE PROPHETIC

#1. HAVING THE RIGHT ATTITUDE

Our perspective towards prophecy should be that of a biblical attitude and the biblical attitude towards prophecy is thoroughly **positive**. Not only are we told to avoid despising prophecy - that is, assigning to it a lesser role than is proper; we are also exhorted to prove all prophecies, and hold fast to what is good and accurate in them (I Thess. 5:20,21). Even more importantly, God commands us to desire earnestly and *covet* the prophetic ministry (I Cor. 12:39; 14:1,39). It is, in fact, the only ministry that the scriptures tell Christians to covet.

A truly inspired personal prophecy is God's specific word to an individual. So the same scriptural principles for the proper attitudes toward the written Logos Word should apply equally to the prophetically spoken rhema word.

Several attitudes are critical for receiving a personal prophecy properly:

FAITH — The basic proper attitude and response towards prophets and personal prophecy is to know and believe that it is scriptural and then receive God's prophetic ministry with faith. Hebrews 11:6 states that without faith it is impossible to please God. If we receive or intend to receive a personal prophecy from a presbytery or a prophet, we should evaluate fully those who might minister prophetically to us. If we conclude that they are qualified, competent men and women of God, then the prophecies should be received in confidence, believing that word to be true and factual. Hence, the attitude of faith is imperative to bring fulfillment. Hebrews 4:2 tells us about the Israelites in the wilderness that "the word preached (prophesied) did not profit them, not being mixed with faith in them that heard it" (Ex. 6 & Heb. 3:17-19). In contrast to the children of Israel, we see Jehoshaphat properly responding with an attitude of faith to the prophetic word delivered by Jahaziel (II Chron. 20). His proper response of faith to his personal prophecy brought his proclamation for God's people to, "Believe in the LORD your God, so shall ye be established; **believe his prophets, so shall ye prosper.**" Jehoshaphat's attitude of faith towards the prophetic word brought great victory (II Chron. 20:22).

If a prophetic word is received with an attitude of acceptance and faith, then the rhema that is heard will create faith for the fulfilling of that word: "So then faith cometh by hearing, and hearing by the word [rhema] of God" (Rom. 10:17).

OBEDIENCE — True faith will always be accompanied by the works of obedience. James 1:22 tells us "Be ye doers of the word, and not hearers only, deceiving your own selves." If our hearing doesn't progress to the point of doing, then we become a candidate for deception.

7

When the Lord chooses to speak a word to us, it isn't just to tickle our intellect, but to bring the understanding necessary to *do* the will of God (Duet.29:29 and Rom.2:13). Therefore, it is actually better not to receive a word at all than to receive one and then not do what the word says <u>to do</u>. "Therefore to him that knoweth to do good and doeth it not, to him it is sin" (James 4:17). If we obey the word and **do** what the word says, then we deliver ourselves from deception and open our spirit and mind to know the will of God. Jesus said, "If any man will do God's will, he shall know...whether it be of God..."(John 7:17). So if we believe and do what we know to do, Christ will speak and reveal more concerning His will for our lives.

As a biblical example of this attitude, we see Noah receiving one prophetic word about building an Ark and because of his obedience, his entire family was saved (Gen. 6). On the other hand, we see King Saul who disobeyed the prophetic word from Samuel (I Sam. 15:24) and

8

reaped the results of loosing the kingship for his lineage.

Thus, the proper attitude of response to personal prophecy requires *obedience*, a cooperation with the word that allows it to have room in our lives for the fulfillment of God's will: "Let the word of Christ dwell in you richly in all wisdom" (Col.3:16).

PATIENCE — Hebrews 6:12 reminds us that it not only takes faith to inherit God's promises but it also takes *patience*. These two qualities enable us to appropriate the prophetic word received until the promise is secured.

After we have received a personal prophecy, and proven it to be a true word from the Lord, we must maintain a constant faith and confidence that it will come to pass regardless of the time required - and that requires **patiently pursuing God's will**. Once we are convinced that a word is a true word quickened by the Holy Spirit, we must allow no one to rob us of it.

I did not understand this principle when I received my first prophecies from a presbytery at the age of nineteen. After leaving college, I settled among Christians who were not familiar with either the prophetic presbytery or personal prophecy. Discouragement came because nothing was happening as quickly as I had expected. I showed the prophecy to a couple of ministers and a friend. They all said they did not witness to it and believed it was a bondage to me. They suggested that I burn it.

In a moment of confusion and discouragement I was ready to cast the prophecies into the flames and destroy all record of their contents. But thank God they were not destroyed, for every one of them has come to pass. They have been a constant source of inspiration, encouragement, and motivation for more than thirty-nine years.

Personal prophecies can be likened to precious pearls! When Jesus said not to cast pearls before swine, He was referring to the Pharisees. He was telling us not to take something God has given us and expose it to religious leaders who do not believe God speaks in personal prophecy today. The devil can and does use well meaning ministers and Christian friends to rob us of our word from the Lord, but we must not let them. Even if our prophecies are causing us confusion, frustration, or discouragement due to the lack of immediate fulfillment, we must nevertheless wait patiently upon the Lord. He will fulfill His prophetic word, changing both us and our circumstances.

I have learned the need and importance of an attitude of patience for persevering during God's prophetic process. When I first came out of Bible college I expected to be launched into worldwide ministry because of the prophecies over me. I expected all those glowing words about being "a leader of leaders" to become an instant reality and I was full of zeal, vision, dedication, and determination. My wrong perception brought pressure and impatience.

I, like many other ministers of that time, was convinced that Jesus was coming any moment. We had no time to waste and I definitely believed that Jesus was going to return before I turned thirty. We could only think in terms of months, not years. Waiting and patience was not part of our vocabulary then; everything had to be done today because there was not going to be any tomorrow. God heard all my prayers to rush the process, but He knew His own timetable and the growing process that would be necessary before all of those prophecies could become manifest in their full demonstration. God is never in a hurry but He is always on time. He is not motivated by intimidation or by our frustration.

My desire was that God's purpose would be perfected in me and I spent several days a month praying by the hour to have His will accomplished in my life. How did God respond to all my pleas? He placed me as the pastor of a small church in the Yakima Valley of Washington State for six years. This church had a history of problems and the remaining congregation had seen it all, been through it all, and knew it all. So they voted in a young pip-squeak prophet to be their pastor with the idea that after all they had been through, they could put up with this young man until he matured some.

For six years God kept me at that church while He continued to make the man rather than manifesting a mighty ministry, which would have crushed me at the time. As with all of us, the ministry could be no greater than the man.

In Psalm 37:7-11 we have a clear biblical admonition for the proper response to personal prophecy, especially those areas that speak of our ministry and the things to be accomplished.

13

In a paraphrased format it could be interpreted to say:

> *"Rest in the Lord, and wait patiently for Him. Commit your way* [the way for your personal prophecies to be fulfilled] *unto the Lord; trust also in Him and He shall bring it* [your personal prophecy] *to pass. Fret not thyself because of him who prospereth in his way* [the person whose ministry is already being fully manifested], *because of the man who bringeth wicked devices to pass* [the minister who is prosperous and successful, yet not righteous in all his ways, doing things his way rather than God's]. *Cease from anger* [at God for not coming through when you wanted Him to], *and forsake wrath* [release your frustrations

and self-imposed pressure to per-
form before God's time]...but
those that wait upon the Lord,
they shall inherit the earth....And
shall delight themselves in the
abundance of peace."

Other scriptures which clarify this divine
principle are Heb.10:35,36; Ps. 27:14; and Is.
40:31. As biblical examples of this attitude, we
see Joseph who received a vision at 17 yet
patiently waited for God's timetable to come to
pass (Gen. 37-42) versus Abraham's impatience
with his prophetic promise for an heir and his
subsequent production of Ishmael (Gen. 15:4;
16:2).

**HUMILITY/ MEEKNESS AND SUB-
MISSION** — Responding properly to a prophetic word requires that the believer receive the
prophetic utterance in a spirit of humility, meekness and submission. If we choose to receive a
true word of prophecy and respond with pride,

anger, doubt, resentment, criticism, self-justification, or arrogance; we reveal immaturity or a wrong spirit. We must be aware that a wrong attitude neutralizes much of what God wants to accomplish by the prophetic words spoken.

Sometimes we have preconceptions about a great ministry we believe God will confirm and describe through the prophet. When God does not confirm our ideas of great self-importance, then we may become disillusioned, depressed and angry at God and the one prophesying. We insist that the prophet or presbytery has missed the mind of God.

We have seen this happen a few times at our prophet seminars where we provide a prophetic presbytery for those who attend. As an example, I remember one particular minister who attended and was unknown to those prophesying. Not one word was mentioned in his presbytery session about him being a great prophet, nor much about the attributes of a prophet.

Later, he came to me complaining that the presbytery had missed it with him because they had
not discerned his great call as a prophet of God.

This man was not manifesting the wisdom
which is from above because he approached me
with an attitude of superiority. He had to be
counselled through his hurt pride and resentment. I patiently and gently dealt with his wrong
spirit and attitude.

Many times, the words which the Lord
speaks to us through prophecy require adjust-
ments in actions and attitudes. James 1:21
states: "Receive with *meekness* the engrafted
word." We must be willing to respond in wisdom. The Bible says that if we rebuke a wise
man, he will be wiser, and if we rebuke a fool,
he will hate us. A mature person with the right
attitude will respond to personal prophecy -
even if it is corrective - with the attributes of
heavenly wisdom: "The wisdom that is from
above is first pure, then peaceable, gentle and

17

easy to be entreated, full of mercy and good fruits, without partiality, and without hypocrisy" (James 3:17). Even if the prophetic word is inaccurate, the righteous and mature person will not respond with carnal or childish behavior.

Finally, **pride** can hinder personal prophecy from coming to pass. A good biblical example is found in II Kings 5 when Captain Naaman of Syria fell ill with leprosy and requested that prophet Elisha heal him. Elisha sent a messenger to Naaman telling him to go to the river Jordan and dip seven times to be healed. Naaman's response was one of anger and outrage for his personal pride was hurt because Elisha had not come to meet him personally and his sense of national pride was hurt because the Jordan river was in Israel rather than in Syria. As the account progressed, Naaman eventually humbled himself to obey Elisha's instructions and his obedience caused the prophetic word of healing to manifest. Again, his willingness to

18

swallow his pride and act with an attitude of obedience activated his prophecy to its fulfillment.

#2. RECORD, READ AND MEDITATE

One of the greatest principles in properly responding to your personal prophecy is to record what was said and write it out so that it may be read and meditated upon. The Apostle Paul told Timothy: "Neglect not the gift that is in thee, which was **given thee by prophecy**, with the laying on of the hands of the presbytery. **Meditate** upon these things; give thyself wholly to them, that thy profiting may appear to all" (I Tim. 4:14,15). Here Paul reminds Timothy that he had been given a gift by prophecy when he was prophesied over by the presbytery. Besides telling him to neglect not the gift within him, Paul also told him to meditate over his personal prophecies so that everything spoken would be made manifest and become profitable to the whole Body of Christ.

This leads to one main question. How could Timothy properly meditate upon those things spoken over him by the prophetic presbytery unless they were written down for him? Obviously, those around Timothy had an understanding of the biblical precedent for recording and meditating upon what God spoke. Such scriptures as Hab. 2:2; Rev. 2:1; Is. 8:1; II Chron. 16:4; Jer. 36:2; Ez. 2:10, 3:1-3; Zech. 5:1-4; Joshua 1:8; Ps. 1:2, 19:14, 39:3, 63:6 validate the importance of recording, writing out and meditating upon God's prophetic word.

In the early days of my ministry (1950's and 1960's) many of the prophecies I received were not recorded because of the lack of sound-recording equipment. Those that I did get on tape were first recorded on a seven-inch-reel wire recorder, and then transferred onto a seven-inch-tape reel. Last, they were written out by hand, and then typed. Today, we can be grateful for the convenience of the cassette recorder and

should always use it for taping personal prophecy.

If we choose not to record prophecy, the
prophecy actually becomes of little value to us
because the important details of the prophetic
word are soon forgotten. This is especially true
if the prophecy is lengthy because the human
mind can only remember a little of the exact
wording. I know this from personal experience;
of the thousands of words that were spoken over
me prophetically but never recorded, I can only
recall two or three phrases. We simply cannot
expect to respond properly to a personal prophecy unless all the words are recorded, read and
understood clearly.

For this reason, all personal prophecies
should be recorded and proper preparation
should be made ahead of time. When an experienced prophetic presbytery is ministering,
they will normally make arrangements to record
everything.

If someone approaches us saying they have a word from the Lord for us, we should ask them to wait a moment until we can get a recorder, or have them come with us to a place where there is recording equipment. If no equipment is available, then ask the person to write the word out so the word can be retained and full benefit can be derived from it. If they are a true man or woman of God, they will honor this request without becoming offended or feeling resentful.

Another benefit of recording a prophetic word is that after receiving several prophecies, they can then be compared for agreement. When comparing, you will usually notice that some of the same thoughts and words appear from the messages of different individuals who were not familiar with what was said to you previously. This agreement helps us realize that they must really be the word of the Lord, because they are being confirmed in the mouth of several witnesses.

Besides benefitting the person who receives a prophetic word, recording also provides personal protection for the prophet. People have a way of misapplying, twisting and reinterpreting what they hear and what they think they hear in a prophecy; so that what they remember conforms to their selfish desires instead of God's will.

As an example, I was once ministering in a church with an unmarried pastor. At the time, I prophesied to a young single woman in the congregation, who several weeks later relayed to Jane, my daughter-in-law, "Did you know that Dr. Hamon prophesied I would marry my pastor?" Jane, questioned her statement and asked whether the woman had written out her prophecy. She had and she showed it to Jane. It read: "God will give you the desires of your heart." Of course, the young woman stated that her desire was to marry her pastor! Jane advised her that she could not assume any marriage plans; but if the prophecy had not

23

been written down, convincing her of that might have been much more difficult. She was not telling people that I prophesied God would give her the desires of her heart but that she should marry her pastor.

Another advantage of recording, writing it out and meditating upon personal prophecies is that it reveals that several interpretations may be possible for the same word. Many times, our first interpretation is not always a true and proper application. I once went to a minister for a prophetic word looking for assurance that God would supply a desperate financial need. At the time, I was two days late on a $40,000 payment and the word of the Lord spoken said, "I will supply your need, for to deny you would be to deny myself." I walked away confessing that my financial need was met, but it never was. Later I went to the Lord inquiring of Him why He hadn't fulfilled His prophetic promise. He replied, "Yes, I did. I met the need I promised prophetically through my servant. *You* thought your greatest need was that payment, but I saw a greater need than that money, and I have met it faithfully." The Lord then gave me revelation so that I could perceive how much greater was the need He *did* meet that night. In light of this example, we should always go over a recorded word from God with a pastor or elder who believes in and understands personal prophecy. Outside objective people can help us make sure that we are not misinterpreting or misapplying the message given.

Last, knowing we must record, read and meditate upon the prophetic word helps restrain us from making any major decisions or drawing any final conclusions about what it means, while it is being given. When receiving a prophetic word, it is best to just listen attentively and prayerfully, reserving all final judgments for later when we have the prophecy before us in written form. At the actual time of receiving a prophetic word, our spirit is best engaged in witnessing actively to the spirit of the person prophesying and the divine inspiration which is motivating him or her, rather than judging and evaluating the prophecy. Proper evaluation can be hindered due to our emotional, mental, and physical posture while receiving a prophecy.

#3. WITNESS TO YOUR PROPHECY

How do we bear witness with a prophetic word's accuracy in spirit and content? The same way we bear witness that we are a child of God: "The Spirit itself beareth witness with our spirit..," (Rom. 8:16). We *prove* prophecy by biblical principles and the proper criteria for judging prophetic words, but we *witness* to a prophecy with our *spirit*.

Sometimes I have heard people say, "I did not witness with that prophecy." But after questioning them, I discovered that what they actually meant was that the prophecy did not confirm their theology, or they did not like what was said, or their emotions reacted negatively to it. They failed to grasp and understand that we do not bear witness with the soulish mind, emotions or will, according to personal opinions, desires or goals.

In order to properly bear witness to a prophetic word, we must be able to discern between our human soul and our spirit. The *spirit realm* of man is where divine love and faith operate; the soul harbors our emotions, reasoning, imagination and soulish desires; and our flesh contains our five senses, including our feeling.

Reasoning is in the mind, not in the spirit. Because of this, our traditions, beliefs and strong opinions are not a true witness to prophetic truth. In fact, these faculties often bring doubt, confusion, resentment, rejection and rebellion against true personal prophecy. Sometimes our head may say "No" while our heart says "Go." Our soul may say, "I don't understand," while our spirit says, "It's fine; don't lean to your own understanding."

27

> *"Trust in the Lord with all thine heart; and lean not unto thine own understanding. In all thy ways acknowledge him, and he shall direct thy paths."*
>
> (Prov.3:5,6)

As an example, consider what would happen if a devout Catholic received a prophecy saying he was not to worship Mary. Would he "bear witness" to that word? Probably not, because of his tradition and his emotional tie to Mary. Likewise, what if you prophesied water baptism by immersion to a Presbyterian or speaking in tongues to a traditional Baptist? You would probably receive the same reaction.

The challenge today is that most people cannot discern between a negative soulish reaction and the spirit's lack of witness to something. The spirit reaction originates deep within our being. Many Christians describe the physical location of its corresponding sensation as a feeling in the upper stomach or lower chest area. A negative spirit-witness, with a message of either "No," "Be careful," or "Something's not right," usually manifests itself with a nervous, jumpy or uneasy feeling, a deep, almost unintelligible sensation that something is not right.

This sensation can only be trusted when we are more in tune with our spirit than with our thoughts. If our thinking is causing these sensations, then it could be a soulish reaction rather than the Spirit bearing a negative witness.

When God's Spirit does bear witness with our spirit that a prophetic word is right, is of God and is according to His divine will and purpose, then our spirit reacts with the fruit of the Holy Spirit. There is a deep, unexplainable peace and joy, a warm, loving feeling or even a sense of our spirit jumping up and down with excitement. This positive sensation assures us that the Holy Spirit is bearing witness with our spirit that everything is in order, even though we may not

29

understand all that is being said, or the soul may not be able to adjust immediately to all the thoughts being presented.

Don't do what you don't witness to. If there is neither reaction nor sensation in the spirit, but rather more of a neutral feeling, then it is a "wait and see" situation. The spirit is saying, "Nothing to get excited about, nothing to get worried about." Time will tell, so we must trust and obey, believe and become, desire and do what we know to do. If the prophecy is of God, it will all come to pass, and we will fulfill God's will.

In closing, to properly bear witness to a prophetic word, we must understand the issue of *new revelation* as opposed to *confirmation* in a prophetic word. Sadly enough, there is a teaching being ministered that prophecy is only for confirmation. In its current form, this teaching insists that we should reject any personal prophecy that presents a thought which is totally new to us. It claims that God will only speak in prophecy things we have already heard from Him in our own spirit, serving merely as confirmation. **This is the ideal but not the real**.

There is no doubt that prophecy is received and borne witness to more easily and immediately when it is a confirmation of things which have already been considered by the person who is receiving the prophecy. But I believe we are seeking a false sense of security when we insist that God will never have a prophet tell us anything unless He has told us first. In fact, I think we are indulging ourselves in a proud ego trip to claim that God must always speak to us first, personally, before He can speak to us through someone else. There is no scripture to support such a belief.

Allow me to give you a few scriptural illustrations revealing that a prophet *can* speak new things to a person from God which that person had never before thought of or considered. For example, *David*, as a young shepherd boy was anointed by Samuel with a prophecy that he would become king. We have no indication that this young man had ever before even dreamed of ruling Israel.

We see *Elisha* as a farmer who had no thoughts of going into ministry until Elijah the prophet revealed that he would be a prophet. *Jehu* had no idea that he might someday be king of Israel until Elijah revealed it to him. *Paul* received his first insight that he would be an apostle to the Gentiles, not from Jesus on the road to Damascus, not from the inward voice of the Holy Spirit, but rather from Ananias when he prophesied the word of the Lord and ministered healing to him.

We cannot reject the word of a prophet or consider it inaccurate simply because we have not already been thinking about what is prophesied. God uses the prophets to speak new truth, not only to the Church, but also to individuals. We must prove all words before rejecting them.

Allow me to give you a personal example before we move onto another principle of response. I once gave a prophetic word to a man in the oil business that he would go into a new business and have a chain of restaurants. At the time, such a thought had never entered into his mind. For four years he stayed in the oil business and forgot about the prophecy. But when the oil business went bad, an opportunity opened up for him to go into the restaurant business - and he is now opening his third restaurant in that chain.

When new thoughts are presented to us in prophecy, we should stay open, write them out, consider them and pray about them. We should wait and see, and remain open, teachable and divinely flexible. When God opens the door of opportunity in the area described, we will already have a confirmation that He is in it. Prophetic confirmations sometimes come before we even know we need one.

#4. WAR A GOOD WARFARE

"This charge I commit unto
thee, son Timothy, *according to
the prophecies which went before
on thee*, that thou by them
mightest war a good warfare."

(I Tim. 1:18)

Paul told Timothy to do more than just meditate upon his prophecies; he said they should be
used to fight the battle! We can take the personal prophecies we have witnessed to and
proven and wage spiritual warfare with them.
The kings of Judah and Israel such as David and
Jehoshaphat, defeated their enemies based upon
personal prophecies they received from a
prophet.

Joshua also received a specific and individual word about Jericho which makes us realize
that prophetic words such as Jehoshaphat's or
Joshua's, gave battle strategy that would work

34

because God said to do it a certain way and at a particular time. This type of word can rightly be called a personal prophecy. These battles were won because the leaders followed specific directions from the Lord for a specific occasion.

Warfare entails perseverance and **personal prophecy gives us the power to persevere**. The Apostle Paul was able to endure great suffering with joy because the man of God had prophesied to him that it was God's will for him to suffer for the name of Christ Jesus.

> *"For I will shew him how great things he must suffer for my name's sake."*
>
> (Acts 9:16)

A good example of waging warfare with prophecy comes from the experience of my wife, Evelyn. In 1979 a prophet gave her a word which contained some things she had not previously thought of, yet she believed the prophet and prospered; she believed God and saw things established.

Part of her prophecy declared that God had made a covenant with her that our children could not and would not marry out of the Lord's will. At the time our two youngest children were not married. Our oldest son, Tim, was already married, and we had all felt an assurance and a witness that Karen was the right one for him. But our second son, twenty-year-old Tom, was going steady with a Christian girl that both my wife and I felt was not the right one. At the same time, Sherilyn, our eighteen-year-old daughter, was planning to marry a solid Christian young man.

Sherilyn's fiance was like a son to us, and we could find no scriptural fault with him. But my wife could not get peace about their marriage. The couple went ahead and set the wedding date, and Evelyn helped Sherilyn choose her wedding dress and make all the wedding preparations.

During this time, my wife was laughing on the outside but crying on the inside because she could not get peace in her spirit about the wedding, even though she mentally agreed to what was happening. She kept quoting and confessing the prophecy she had received that her children would not marry out of God's will. She repeated privately to the Lord, "God, you gave me a personal prophetic promise that you had made a covenant with me while my children were still in the womb that none of them would marry the wrong person. I did not know that before, Lord, but since you revealed it I am believing your prophet and you, God, for my children to prosper and be established in marriage with your preordained helpmate."

Sherilyn's wedding date was set for August 16, 1980. The four of us left in June to itinerate in ministry up till two weeks before the wedding. Everything was set; all that remained was to have the ceremony.

The providential events that followed would require in themselves a whole book to describe. But to tell the story briefly, near the end of our itinerary we arrived in DeFuniak Springs, Florida, where the pastor, Glenn Miller, was a twenty-five-year-old single man engaged to be married himself. On the second night of the meetings God spoke separately and independently to Sherilyn and Glenn, telling her, "That's your husband," and telling him, "That's your wife." So both of them broke their engagements and became engaged to each other.

As it turned out, we all ended up back in Phoenix, Arizona, where we lived at the time, and we went ahead and had the wedding - but with a different groom!

Meanwhile, Tom had broken off his steady relationship with that young lady, had met another beautiful blonde in Bible college, and became engaged to her. I am convinced that their eventual marriage resulted in part because Evelyn had done warfare with her prophecy. All our children are now married in the perfect will of God, with mates God ordained for them. They are prospering greatly and have given us nine beautiful grandchildren.

Yes, we can take our proven personal prophecy as a word from the Lord and war a warfare with it that will cause everything to work according to the perfect will of God. If we believe God, we will be established, but we must also believe His prophets in order to prosper (II Chron. 20:20).

#5. DO NOTHING DIFFERENT UNLESS DEFINITELY DIRECTED

When an individual receives a personal prophecy and it contains such references as what God is going to do in the person's life, the call of God on their life, etc., what should that person do? For an example, a young man who is committed to Christ and is studying to be a lawyer in law school receives a personal prophecy that says he is called to pastor. Should he quit law school and go into the ministry, should he finish his secular degree, or should he change his major to pastoral studies? Considering the many options, how should he respond to the word given?

My best advice according to biblical pattern is to **do nothing different unless definitely directed**. Unless God gives us explicit instructions to act upon, the proper response to personal prophecy is simply to continue doing what we have been doing before we received the word of the Lord. This is true even if we have been told of great things we will do in the future!

As an example, we see that David was called from tending sheep, and Samuel anointed him to be king over all Israel. But there were no prophetic indications about when or how this was to come to pass, nor any instructions for David to follow. It was simply a prophetic proclamation. So David returned to his ministry of tending sheep, practicing with his slingshot, and learning to sing and play music to the Lord. Since he was in his early teens at the time, there was nothing he could do about his personal prophecy of kingship except to wait upon God's timing and to occupy his time profitably while he dreamed about his day of prophetic fulfillment (I Sam.16). For all true prophecies of future accomplishments - ours as well - God's time for fulfillment must be awaited.

On the other hand, when a prophecy is received which includes specific instructions and an anointing for immediate action, then it is time to act upon the prophecy (II Kings 9). As an example, Jehu, one of the chief captains of the army of Israel, received such a prophecy. Elisha commissioned one of his young prophets to take a box of anointing oil and go to Ramoth-

41

Gilead, where he was to anoint Jehu king of Israel, and then run. The young man not only anointed Jehu king, but also prophesied the destruction of the Ahab dynasty, which Elijah had also prophesied to Jehu some twelve years earlier (II Kings 9:8,9; I Kings 21).

Jehu's years of experience had prepared him for this time. He was zealous for the Lord, willing and ready. All his fellow captains witnessed with his decision. So God's timing caused everything to fall in order, enabling and encouraging him to act immediately upon the prophecy and to follow through until he had fulfilled faithfully all that had been spoken (II Kings 9,10).

Jehu and David reveal the two possible responses to a prophetic word. Jehu *took immediate action* to fulfill his prophecy and was launched into a twenty-eight year reign as king of Israel. David on the other hand, *did nothing immediately* to fulfill his prophecy, but waited patiently approximately seventeen years before it was even partially fulfilled, and another seven before fulfillment was complete. His patient waiting **without trying to make the prophecy come to pass on his own strength** ultimately launched him into a successful kingship ministry of forty years.

#6. UNDERSTANDING GOD'S UNIVERSAL DIVINE PRINCIPLES

God has divine requirements, directives, and principles that must be in operation in order for anything that He has established to work. Just as there are natural laws in the universe and in nature, so there are biblical/ spiritual laws for obtaining and fulfilling your personal and ministerial needs.

For water to be formed, there has to be the right combination of hydrogen and oxygen (H_2O). For an airplane to fly, it must have the right design and thrust. It must conform to the laws of aerodynamics in order to overcome the law of gravity so that it can take off, maintain a controlled flight, and then make a successful landing. Personal prophecy is like the airplane, our ability to accomplish and fulfill what was spoken is dependent upon certain laws.

As an example, imagine if someone gave you a car to make a trip across the country. Does having the car guarantee that you will get there? NO! You, as the driver, have a part to play in order to make sure that the car fulfills its mission. You must keep gas in the gas tank, oil in the engine, water in the radiator, fix any flat tires, etc. Just because you received a personal prophecy that revealed things you were to be and do and arrive at a certain destination of personal and ministerial accomplishment, does not guarantee that it will take you there. You must keep your "car" full of the gas of faith and obedience, maintain the right amount of oil of peaceful trust, and keep the proper level of water of joyful expectation.

Fulfilling personal prophecy is like baking a cake. All the necessary ingredients must be put together in proper proportion, blended together to the right consistency, and then baked in the oven the proper amount of time. Only then will it have the shape and taste that others would desire to receive and partake of.

Fulfilling personal prophecy is also like getting your prayers answered. Jesus declared that we are to "ask and ye shall receive" and "whatsoever you ask the Father in My name that shall you receive" (John 15:24; 16:23). Yet many Christians "ask" in prayer for many things and never receive them. Does that make the words of Jesus false or inaccurate because Christians quote those scriptures and then ask but nothing happens? Shall we throw those scriptures out and say they are not of God because they didn't come to pass like we expected? NO! For answered prayer, like the cake, has many more ingredients than the aspect of just "asking."

45

For instance, James declares, "Ye ask and receive not, because ye ask amiss, that ye may consume it upon your lusts" (James 4:3). Here we find the additional ingredients, asking for the right thing with the proper motive. Other scriptures, such as Mark 11:24 and Heb. 11:6, reveal that "faith" must be added to our prayers in order for them to be answered.

Likewise, the same is true for personal prophecy. There are certain attitudes and actions that must be blended together and then left in the oven of God's timing before it can be fulfilled properly. Just as the car is not at fault for not taking you to your desired destination if you don't maintain it, personal prophecy will not be fulfilled unless we learn how to properly respond to God's voice.

In other prophetic booklets, we give you additional insight and understanding in the area of personal prophecy. This booklet dealt with the main ingredients that are needed to fulfill personal prophecy. Like growing corn, we dealt with the seed type and soil type necessary to grow corn (personal prophecy). In one of our booklets entitled, **Hindrances to Personal Prophecy,** we reveal the things that we and others can do that can cause our corn (personal prophecies) to be hindered from reaching fruition. All personal prophecies are conditional. There are many things that keep corn from reaching maturity and harvest: watering, storms, cut-worms, blight, diseases, animals breaking into the field and devouring, or the farmer impatiently reaping before the corn is ready for the harvest. Many examples, using the lives of biblical characters, are utilized in the above booklet to show the things that can cause personal prophecies to be hindered, perverted, or completely canceled.

In conclusion, memorize and meditate upon these proper responses to personal prophecy until they are incorporated into your life and ministry. Believe God so that you will be estab-

47

lished and believe your personal prophecies and war a good warfare with them so that you may prosper and be victorious in your Christian life and ministry.

From these six prophetic guidelines we can conclude that it is not enough to receive a prophecy. We must also respond properly in order to see its fulfillment. To review these six, **we must**:

1. Have the right attitudes of faith, obedience, patience, humility, meekness and submission.

2. Be willing to record, read and meditate upon the prophetic words we have received.

3. Learn to properly discern so that we may bear witness to our prophecies.

4. Be willing to war a good warfare.

5. Do nothing different unless we are definitely directed.

6. Understand God's universal divine principles.

BOOKS BY DR. BILL HAMON

Prophets and Personal Prophecy Vol. I   **$9.95**
God's Prophetic Voice Today   *240 pgs.*
Within this best selling book are the guidelines for receiving, understanding and fulfilling God's personal word to you. This book makes incredible strides towards restoring personal prophecy to the Church and is the only book of its kind.

Prophets and the Prophetic Movement Vol. 2.   **$.9.95**
God's Prophetic Move Today   *252 pgs.*
This book is the second in a series on understanding and restoring the ministry of the prophet and the prophetic with biblical integrity and balance. This book presents an overview of the current move of God, its purpose and place in Church history and the truths and ministries being restored.

Prophets, Pitfalls and Principles Vol. 3   **$9.95**
God's Prophetic People Today   *238 pgs.*
This third book has been described as a "must for all prophets and Christian leaders." Foreworded by Oral Roberts, it covers four important areas: The pitfalls we must avoid as a prophetic people, the priciples we must practice, the 10 M's for determining true prophets and last, a look at prophetic end-time events. This volume is a must for those who plan to press on, with integrity and balance, in the prophetic ministry.

The Eternal Church   *422 pgs.*   *$9.95*
An exciting panoramic view of God's eternal purposes in Church restoration over the past 500 years with special emphasis on the current move of the Holy Spirit and what is next on God's agenda.

*To order your personal copy
of these exciting books,
see the order sheet on the last page!!*

Prophetic
PIT FALLS
Character flaws, Weed seeds and Root problems

The Tape Series...

This tape series will **enhance and amplify** the material covered in **Prophets, Principles and Pitfalls,** Vol. 3 with **more** examples, illustrations and vital information included.

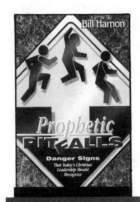

- *Prophet Elijah Pitfall*
- *Jeremiah, Ezekiel and Abraham Pitfall*
- *Prophet Moses Pitfall*
- *Prophet Johab Pitfall*
- *James and John Syndrome*
- *Achan and Judas Pitfall*
- *Balaam Pitfall*

This exciting seven tape series is an in-depth look at the pitfalls that face today's Christians. Dr. Hamon used biblical characters to disclose the subtle satanic pitfalls which can cause leadership and saints to fall. **This tape series is a must for Christian leadership!**

7 Tape Series ONLY $30.00

Please refer to the last page in this book to order your set of *"Prophetic Pitfalls"*.

PROPHETIC PRAISE TAPES

The God of Glory Thunders tape embodies the spirit of warfare in worship. Taking you from the height of **exuberant high praises** to the glories of the **melodic sounds of intimate worship** before the Lrod. There is truly a powerful anointing that permeates the worship experience of this tape.

Pastor Tom Hamon, Christian International Center
Santa Rosa Beach, Florida

There is a new sound on the horizon. It's the sound of war as the Lion of the Tribe of Judah begins to Roar through His people. This tape will invite you to join in the high praises of God, make prophetic declarations in song, and execute the vengeance of God on the principalities and powers of the air.

As I worshipped with the tape, I experienced the prophetic revelation and reality of Jesus being manifested as the "Mighty Man of War" in the midst of the worshipping congregation."

Greg Railey, Apostle, Psalmist
President New Song Ministries
Columbia, South Carolina

Lead Sheets and Sound Tracks also available.

NETWORK OF
PROPHETIC
MINISTRIES

*"Providing preparation and place for
prophets and prophetic ministry."*

The CI-NPM is an international association of prophetic ministers founded by Bishop Hamon to provide training, equipping and accountability based on relationship.

The particular purpose of CI-NPM is:

■ to see the **OFFICE OF THE PROPHET FULLY RESTORED** within the Church to the level of acceptance and recognition that the pastor, evangelist and teacher have today.

■ to **TEACH, TRAIN and ACTIVATE** the prophets given to our charge so that they are equipped for **mature, accurate** ministry within the Body of Christ and to the world.

The **SPECIFIC MISSION** God has given us to facilitate these goals are:

■ to be a **CENTRAL HEADQUARTERS** for gathering, uniting, covering and sending forth of **PROPHETIC MINISTERS.**

■ to be a **VITAL RESOURCE CENTER** for books, teaching tapes, workbooks, magazines, videos and other materials needed to propagate the prophetic ministry.

■ to **CONDUCT REGIONAL PROPHETS CONFERENCES** throughout the U.S. and the nations of the world to introduce and take the prophetic ministry into every region of the world.

■ to see the **PROPHETIC PASTORS TRAIN THEIR LEADER-SHIP INTO PROPHETIC TEAMS** who minister the gifts and grace of God to edify the Church and to convert the lost by demonstrating the reality of God's love and power.

*Drawing from her **real life experiences** in family ministry, **Evelyn, Dr. Hamon's wife,** shares **wisdom and insight** from God's Word. She offers **encouragement and practical application** in...*

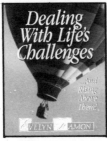

Including:

- Principles of Progress/Promotion
- Spiritual Seasons
- Divine Flexibility
- Maintaining a Positive Attitude

Including:

- Growing Through Stages in God
- Determination in Destiny
- Sharing on Family Life in Ministry
- Straight Talk on Husband/Wife Relationships

Each set is a **4 Tape Series ONLY $20.00**

Please refer to the last page in this book to order your very own set of
Dealing with Life's Callenges and *Handling Life's Realities,*

Order CI-NPM Prophetic Materials Today

Books by Dr. Bill Hamon
The Eternal Church .... $ 9.95
Prophets and Personal Prophecy .... $. 9.95
   Teaching Manual $39.95
   Workbook $25.00
Prophets and the Prophetic Movement .... $ 9.95
Prophets Pitfalls and Principles .... $ 9.95

Books by Evelyn Hamon
The Spiritual Seasons of Life .... $ 2.95

Teaching Tape Series
Prophetic Pitfalls (Dr. Bill Hamon) $30.00
The 10 M's (Dr. Bill Hamon) $15.00
Plugging Into your Gifts $30.00
Handling Life's Realities (Evelyn Hamon) $20.00
Dealing With Life's Challenges (Evelyn Hamon) .. $20.00

Prophetic Praises Cassette Tapes
Mighty Man of War .... $ 8.95
Roar Lion of Judah .... $ 8.95
   CD $12.95
The God of Glory Thunders .... $ 8.95
Lead Sheets and Sound Tracks available for each title:
   Lead Sheets .... $ 5.00
   Sound Tracks $11.95

Other Materials
Personal Prophecies Notebook $12.95
Various video titles available, ask for our **FREE** Prophetic
Resouces Catalog.

To order call: (904) 231-5308 or 1-800-388-5308
   Have Your MasterCard or Visa ready when you call.

or write:

Christian International

P.o. Box 9000

Santa Rosa Beach, Fl. 32459-9000

Enclose check or money order, include $3.00 postage and handling.

Fulfilling Your Personal Prophecy

Pastors, make sure all of your leadership and members have their own copy of this vital booklet.

Everyone needs this book, who thinks they have received a personal word from God.

Buy in quantity and give one to each person who receives a Personal Prophecy through your ministry.

SPECIAL VOLUME DISCOUNTS

Number of Copies	Price Per Copy	Approximate % Discount
1	$2.95	
2 to 10	$2.25	25% Discount
11 to 99	$1.75	44% Discount
100+	$1.25	60% Discount

MUST BE PURCHASED IN **FULL BOXES** OF 100 PER BOX
(**$125.00** PER BOX OF 100 BOOKS)